STEM
ON THE BATTLEFIELD

CODES, CIPHERS, AND CARTOGRAPHY
MATH GOES TO WAR

Terry Burrows

Lerner Publications ◆ Minneapolis

Lerner Publications Company
A division of Lerner Publishing Group, Inc.
241 First Avenue North
Minneapolis, MN 55401 USA

For reading levels and more information, look up this title at www.lernerbooks.com.

Main body text set in Verdana Regular 11/16.5.
Typeface provided by Microsoft.

Picture Credits:
Front cover © Department of Defense.
Interior: USN Art Collection, 4; Library of Congress 5; NMB, 6; Yellow Street Photos, 7; iStock/Thinkstock, 8; Department of Defense, 9, 10; Library of Congress, 11, 12; Robert Hunt Library, 13; Library of Congress, 14cr; Christopher Wood/Shutterstock, 14bl; Luringen, 15; LiveAuctioneers, 16; Brandon T. Fields, 17; National Archives, 18; iStock/Thinkstock, 19; University of Oklahoma Libraries, 20; Department of Defense, 21, 22; Robert Hunt Library, 23, 24; interfoto/Mary Evans Picture Library, 25; Matt Crypto, 26; Robert Hunt Library, 27; Gordon Bell/Shutterstock, 28; famouspeople/Alamy, 29tr; Robert Hunt Library, 29b; National Security Agency, 30; Robert Hunt Library, 31; Leo Blanchette/Shutterstock, 32; Robert Hunt Library, 33; National Archives, 34; Robert Hunt Library, 35tr; Nyvit-art/Shutterstock, 35b; Robert Hunt Library, 36; National Archives, 37; US Navy, 38/39; Robert Hunt Library, 38br, 40; Department of Defense, 41; Robert Hunt Library, 42; iStock/Thinkstock, 43.

Brown Bear Books has made every attempt to contact the copyright holder.
If you have any information please contact licensing@brownbearbooks.co.uk

Library of Congress Cataloging-in-Publication Data

Names: Burrows, Terry, 1963–
Title: Codes, ciphers, and cartography : math goes to war / Terry Burrows.
Description: Minneapolis : Lerner Publications, [2018] | Series: STEM on the battlefield | Audience: Age 9–12. | Audience: Grade 4 to 6. | Includes bibliographical references and index.
Identifiers: LCCN 2017002408 (print) | LCCN 2017008464 (ebook) | ISBN 9781512439274 (lb : alk. paper) | ISBN 9781512449495 (eb pdf)
Subjects: LCSH: Ciphers—Juvenile literature. | Cryptography—Juvenile literature. | Cartography—Juvenile literature. | World War, 1939–1945—Cryptography—Juvenile literature.
Classification: LCC Z103.3 .B87 2018 (print) | LCC Z103.3 (ebook) | DDC 652/.8—dc23

LC record available at https://lccn.loc.gov/2017002408

Manufactured in the United States of America
1-42140-25413-4/19/2017

CONTENTS

MATH AT WAR

In June 1942, Japanese naval commanders saw a chance to destroy the US Navy in the Pacific Ocean. Six months earlier, the Japanese had attacked the US fleet at Pearl Harbor. Japan planned to draw the remaining US ships into a trap. The Japanese would launch a surprise attack at Midway Island. But they did not know that the Americans were waiting for them. US experts had cracked Japan's secret naval codes and knew the attack at Midway was coming. On June 4, the United States attacked the Japanese. In the three-day battle, they sank four Japanese aircraft carriers. The Japanese navy never recovered from the defeat.

An American torpedo bomber climbs away from a burning Japanese ship during the Battle of Midway.

American code breakers were mathematicians who changed the course of warfare. Armies have always used codes to keep their plans secret from the enemy—and the enemy has always tried to break those codes. Mathematics is the basis of modern code breaking.

George Cayley's principles of flight led to the first powered flight by the Wright Brothers at Kitty Hawk, North Carolina, in 1903.

RANGE OF USES

Math has also had many other uses in military history. Geometry, or the study of shapes, was the basis of **navigation** at sea. **Surveyors** used geometry to map unknown territory. With the development of **artillery**, mathematics allowed gunners to figure out the range of targets. In the late eighteenth century, George Cayley used math to figure out the principles of flight.

In the late twentieth century, math became the basis for all computers. Computers became widely used in weaponry. And military computers are likely to dramatically change warfare in the future as well.

NAVIGATION

Navigation is the science of planning and following a route. For centuries, sailors had no way to chart their course other than to use math to figure out their location.

In the third century BCE, the Greek mathematician Eratosthenes had the idea of placing an imaginary grid around the Earth. The grid had lines running from north to south, and from east to west. In around 120 BCE, a Greek astronomer named Hipparchus used math to plot locations on these lines. He used a method modern mathematicians call triangulation.

Early ships, like this Phoenician galley, usually stayed close to shore, so sailors could navigate by using landmarks on the coast.

Triangulation is based on the idea that someone who knows the length and angles of one side of a triangle can figure out the length of the other two sides.

MEASURING LATITUDE

A position north or south on Earth is called latitude. A position from east to west is called longitude. Sailors found their latitude by measuring the angle of the sun or stars above the horizon. They then used a version of triangulation to figure out their position on the globe. Sailors measured the angle of the sun or stars in degrees of **elevation**. The first sailors held out their arms and used their fingers as a rough measure. In the ninth century, Arabian navigators invented a device called a kamal. The kamal used knots in a string to measure angles.

Dead Reckoning

Before it was possible to measure longitude, sailors used dead reckoning to calculate their position. This method was based on the ship's last known position, called a fix. The sailors used their speed, direction, and how long they had been sailing to figure out their new position. If one fix was wrong, however, later fixes became even more inaccurate. On a long voyage, sailors might think they were hundreds of miles from their true position.

The kamal was a piece of wood with a knotted string. One of the knots was held in the teeth and the kamal was held out at arm's length. Matching up the edges of the board with a known star and the horizon gave the sailor his latitude.

In the 1750s, the English mathematician John Bird invented the sextant. This instrument measured the angle between any two objects. It helped sailors calculate latitude accurately.

MARINE CHRONOMETER

From the late fifteenth century, the ships of Europe's navies explored the world. Europeans set up new trade routes and colonies, or overseas settlements. Sailors needed a way to measure longitude. For this, they needed to know the exact time. Most clocks and watches kept time poorly on sea voyages. The problem was solved in 1735. The Englishman John Harrison built an accurate watch called a marine chronometer. It compared the time on the ship with the time in London. That helped sailors figure out their position by studying the position of the sun. For the first time, precise seafaring navigation was possible.

USING RADIO

In the late nineteenth century, naval commanders began to use radio for navigation. Scientists invented a Radio Direction Finder (RDF) before World War I (1914–1918). Ships and aircraft carried a special antenna. The antenna picked up signals from two different radio posts. The RDF used the signals to do triangulation. This calculation helped engineers to figure out the position of the ship or aircraft. Radio was the main means of sea and air navigation during the twentieth century.

Engineers working for the US Army test updated Radio Direction Finder equipment in 1929. The round device is an antenna for receiving radio signals.

GPS

In 1974 the first Global Positioning System (GPS) satellites were launched into space. GPS satellites broadcast a continuous signal that is picked up by receivers on board ships. The GPS identifies a ship's precise location. These days even the smallest of sea vessels carries GPS.

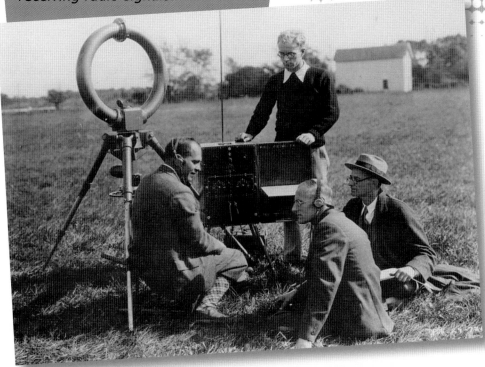

MILITARY CARTOGRAPHY

On the battlefield, generals use features of the landscape to help defeat the enemy. Hills may help shelter their men, valleys may be used to trap the enemy, and rivers may cut off the enemy's route of retreat.

The basis of military planning is cartography, or the drawing of maps. Battles are often fought in places that are unfamliar to military commanders. Satellite photographs of nearly every part of Earth's surface are now available, but in the past military surveyors had to draw maps of battlefields using triangulation to figure out distance, the height of hills, and the width of rivers.

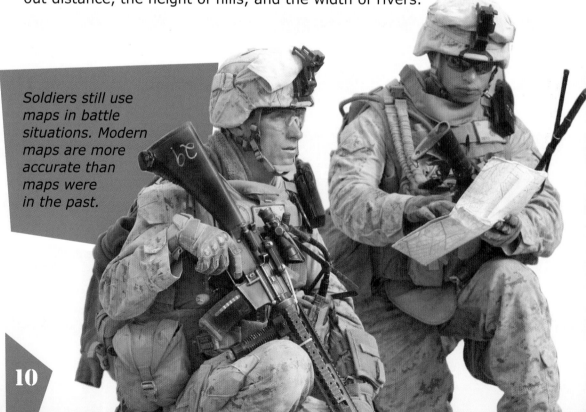

Soldiers still use maps in battle situations. Modern maps are more accurate than maps were in the past.

Military cartographers are mapmakers who create maps to help plan battle tactics. This is first known to have happened in 1813, during the Napoleonic Wars (1803–1815). The Prussians fought Emperor Napoleon of France at Leipzig in Germany. Prussian surveyors made maps to plan their attack. Using their knowledge of the local area, the Prussian military defeated Napoleon. It was his first serious defeat in 10 years of fighting other European powers.

Into the West

The US Army Corps of Topographical Engineers was set up in 1838 to survey the West, much of which was then unexplored. The Corps looked for sites to build forts and other military facilities. The members of the Corps were skilled mappers. They surveyed the landscape to decide the best routes for trails, roads, and railroads.

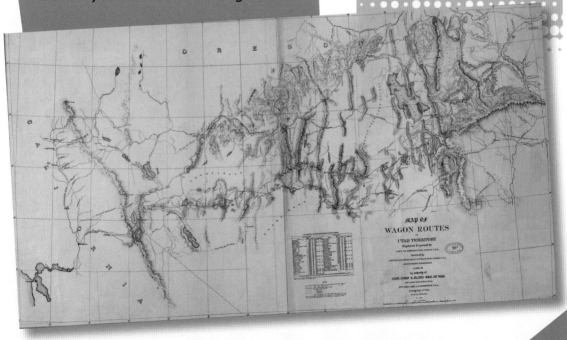

Captain James H. Simpson of the Corps of Topographical Engineers created this map in 1859. It shows wagon routes across Utah used by the US Army and settlers heading West.

GEOGRAPHICAL ADVANTAGE

Military maps record any information that might help troops, from the **climate** to the type of ground in an area. During the Civil War (1861–1865), Union and Confederate forces clashed in the Battle of Gettysburg in Pennsylvania in 1863. Union surveyors advised commanders to position their soldiers on hard, rocky ground above the town of Gettysburg. The Confederates advanced uphill across soft ground, which slowed them down, making them easy to shoot. The Union victory was a turning point in the war.

On this map of the Gettysburg battlefield, the pale blue areas (left) mark the positions of Union troops on the second day of the battle, occupying high ground overlooking the town.

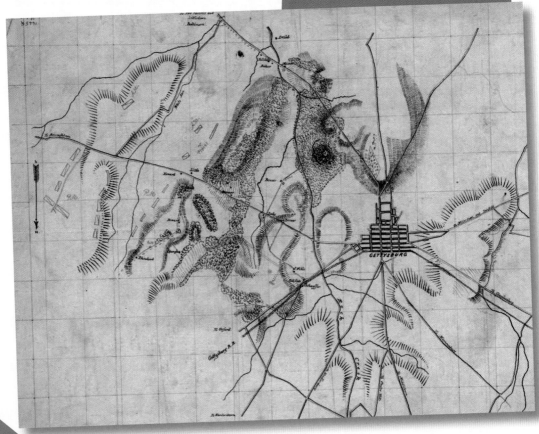

AIR PHOTOGRAPHY

Big advances in military cartography came with the development of the camera in the nineteenth century and the invention of the airplane in 1903. In World War I pilots took photographs of enemy positions. Army commanders used the photographs to plan attacks. In the Vietnam War (1955–1975), the US Army Map Service used aerial photographs to map parts of Vietnam, some of which had not been mapped before.

A photographer in the US Army Air Force in World War I. US aerial observers could deliver a photograph to Army commanders within 20 minutes of it being taken.

These days, satellites orbit the Earth. They continuously photograph the planet. Military mapmakers use the images to create accurate maps of war zones. These maps were used by US forces in Afghanistan and Iraq in the 2000s.

CODES AND CIPHERS

In warfare, it is essential to keep military plans secret. Codes and ciphers are ways to disguise messages. They make it difficult for the enemy to learn information.

Codes and ciphers work in different ways. A code converts a written message into a different form. One example is Morse code. It replaces letters in a message with patterns of dots and dashes. Another form of code might be raising or lowering a window blind as a sign. In a cipher, letters are replaced by other letters or numbers.

THE BRAINS

Samuel Morse (1791–1872) developed a method of sending wireless messages. Morse Code encoded letters and numbers as dots and dashes. These short or long signals could be heard as clicks or bleeps or seen as flashing lights. The Morse code for "S-O-S"— three dots, three dashes, three dots—is still the most widely used international distress signal.

MORSE CODE

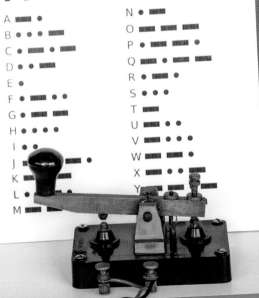

A ▬ •
B • • • •
C • ▬ • ▬
D • • ▬
E •
F • ▬ • •
G ▬ ▬ •
H • • • •
I • •
J • ▬ ▬ ▬
K ▬ • ▬
L • ▬ • •
M ▬ ▬

N • ▬
O ▬ ▬ ▬
P • ▬ ▬ •
Q ▬ ▬ • ▬
R • ▬ •
S • • •
T ▬
U • • ▬
V • • • ▬
W • ▬ ▬
X ▬ • • ▬
Y ▬ • ▬ ▬

Morse code was tapped out using a small telegraph key, which sent long or short electrical pulses along telegraph wires to stand for dashes and dots.

14

The letters on the ancient Greek scytale matched up when they were wound around a rod.

In both codes and ciphers, the original message is called plaintext. Turning the message into code or cipher is known as encryption.

The first people to use codes in warfare were the Spartans of ancient Greece. In the fifth century BCE, Spartan commanders used a device called a scytale to communicate. They wrapped a long strip of tape in a spiral around a rod. Then they wrote a message on the tape. A messenger unwound the tape to carry the message. The message could only be read when the tape was wound back around a rod.

THE CAESAR CIPHER

In the first century BCE, the ancient Romans created a simple type of cipher. They shifted the letters of a message along the alphabet by a set number. Moving five letters on from *D*, for example, gives the letter *I*. The word *DOG* becomes *ITL*. This cipher is called the Caesar Cipher. It was named for the general (and later, emperor) Julius Caesar, who used the cipher to send orders to his generals.

ROTATING DISKS

In the fifteenth century, an Italian architect named Leon Battista Alberti developed a more complex cipher. This used a disk with another rotating disk inside it. Alberti wrote letters on the two disks. The user turned the inner disk a set number of places for each letter, then replaced the letter with the letter alongside it on the outer disk.

This cipher disk from the Civil War is marked CSA, for the Confederate States of America. The outer wheel was turned to encrypt and read the message.

Civil War Codes

During the US Civil War, both sides created cipher disks. The Union Signal Disk was made from cardboard. The inner and outer disks both displayed 30 cells of letters and numbers. The Confederate cipher disk was simpler. It was made from brass and used just the 26 letters of the alphabet.

	A	B	C	D	E	F	G	H	I	J	K	L	M	N	O	P	Q	R	S	T	U	V	W	X	Y	Z
A	A	B	C	D	E	F	G	H	I	J	K	L	M	N	O	P	Q	R	S	T	U	V	W	X	Y	Z
B	B	C	D	E	F	G	H	I	J	K	L	M	N	O	P	Q	R	S	T	U	V	W	X	Y	Z	A
C	C	D	E	F	G	H	I	J	K	L	M	N	O	P	Q	R	S	T	U	V	W	X	Y	Z	A	B
D	D	E	F	G	H	I	J	K	L	M	N	O	P	Q	R	S	T	U	V	W	X	Y	Z	A	B	C
E	E	F	G	H	I	J	K	L	M	N	O	P	Q	R	S	T	U	V	W	X	Y	Z	A	B	C	D
F	F	G	H	I	J	K	L	M	N	O	P	Q	R	S	T	U	V	W	X	Y	Z	A	B	C	D	E
G	G	H	I	J	K	L	M	N	O	P	Q	R	S	T	U	V	W	X	Y	Z	A	B	C	D	E	F
H	H	I	J	K	L	M	N	O	P	Q	R	S	T	U	V	W	X	Y	Z	A	B	C	D	E	F	G
I	I	J	K	L	M	N	O	P	Q	R	S	T	U	V	W	X	Y	Z	A	B	C	D	E	F	G	H
J	J	K	L	M	N	O	P	Q	R	S	T	U	V	W	X	Y	Z	A	B	C	D	E	F	G	H	I
K	K	L	M	N	O	P	Q	R	S	T	U	V	W	X	Y	Z	A	B	C	D	E	F	G	H	I	J
L	L	M	N	O	P	Q	R	S	T	U	V	W	X	Y	Z	A	B	C	D	E	F	G	H	I	J	K
M	M	N	O	P	Q	R	S	T	U	V	W	X	Y	Z	A	B	C	D	E	F	G	H	I	J	K	L
N	N	O	P	Q	R	S	T	U	V	W	X	Y	Z	A	B	C	D	E	F	G	H	I	J	K	L	M
O	O	P	Q	R	S	T	U	V	W	X	Y	Z	A	B	C	D	E	F	G	H	I	J	K	L	M	N
P	P	Q	R	S	T	U	V	W	X	Y	Z	A	B	C	D	E	F	G	H	I	J	K	L	M	N	O
Q	Q	R	S	T	U	V	W	X	Y	Z	A	B	C	D	E	F	G	H	I	J	K	L	M	N	O	P
R	R	S	T	U	V	W	X	Y	Z	A	B	C	D	E	F	G	H	I	J	K	L	M	N	O	P	Q
S	S	T	U	V	W	X	Y	Z	A	B	C	D	E	F	G	H	I	J	K	L	M	N	O	P	Q	R
T	T	U	V	W	X	Y	Z	A	B	C	D	E	F	G	H	I	J	K	L	M	N	O	P	Q	R	S
U	U	V	W	X	Y	Z	A	B	C	D	E	F	G	H	I	J	K	L	M	N	O	P	Q	R	S	T
V	V	W	X	Y	Z	A	B	C	D	E	F	G	H	I	J	K	L	M	N	O	P	Q	R	S	T	U
W	W	X	Y	Z	A	B	C	D	E	F	G	H	I	J	K	L	M	N	O	P	Q	R	S	T	U	V
X	X	Y	Z	A	B	C	D	E	F	G	H	I	J	K	L	M	N	O	P	Q	R	S	T	U	V	W
Y	Y	Z	A	B	C	D	E	F	G	H	I	J	K	L	M	N	O	P	Q	R	S	T	U	V	W	X
Z	Z	A	B	C	D	E	F	G	H	I	J	K	L	M	N	O	P	Q	R	S	T	U	V	W	X	Y

This sheet lays out letters for using a Vigenère cipher. It allows the coder to figure out which letter to substitute for the original by using the vertical and horizontal axes to see the letter where the lines meet.

MORE COMPLEXITY

In 1553 the Italian Giovan Battista Bellaso developed another cipher. It used a number of Caesar ciphers at the same time. The number of letters to be moved backward or forward was set by using a **keyword**. At the time, people thought this cipher was impossible to crack. It became known as the Vigenère cipher because it was mistakenly said to have been invented by the Frenchman Blaise de Vigenère in the nineteenth century.

Over time ciphers became increasingly sophisticated. Some used many alphabets at the same time. In the 1920s machines used **geared** wheels to generate ciphers. Modern-day ciphers use computers. Without knowing the key, these ciphers are almost impossible to crack.

CODE BREAKING

In war, being able to read enemy messages can mean the difference between victory and defeat. Code breaking has changed the course of wars.

During World War I, the German government sent a telegram to its ambassador in Mexico. The message was in cipher. It told the German ambassador to ask Mexico for help in the war. In return, Germany offered to give Mexico land in the southern United States if Germany won the war. The British intercepted the message and broke the code. They showed the message to the Americans, who were outraged. The telegram was one reason the United States decided to enter the war against Germany in April 1917.

The British intercepted this secret telegram from Germany in January 1917. It is known as the Zimmermann Telegram, after the German foreign secretary of the time.

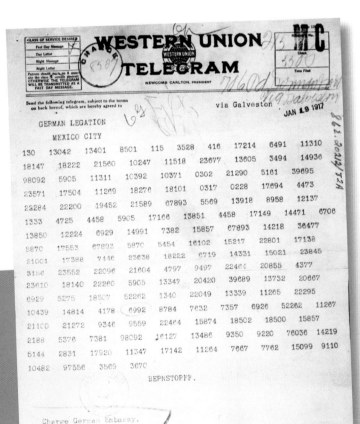

NEW METHODS

In the ninth century, an Arabian scholar named Al-Kindi described a method for reading ciphers. His method is called frequency analysis. The method compares how often letters appear in the cipher with the most common letters in a language.

Ciphers using more than one alphabet were more difficult to break. In 1863 Friedrich Kasiski broke the Vigenère cipher. He worked out the length of the keyword. Then he tried different strings of letters in its place until one worked. Testing strings of letters in this way would be simple for a modern computer.

In the twentieth century, counting machines became important in code breaking. Some modern military ciphers are unbreakable unless the code breaker learns information such as the keyword.

SCIENCE FILE

Frequency Analysis

The number of times letters or groups of letters occur in a language is key for breaking a cipher. In English, e is the most common letter. The letter that appears most in the cipher probably stands for e. In the same way, *th* is the most common letter pairing. Code breakers look out for repeated letters in a cipher that might stand for *th*.

Computers made it possible to make more complicated codes. Code breaking became even more difficult when the military began using computers.

BALLISTICS

Ballistics is the study of bullets and missiles. Missiles are usually fired from guns and cannons. Experts use math to figure out how far they will fly.

Ancient warriors knew that in order to throw a spear farther, they had to throw it harder. This allowed the spear to travel farther before it slowed down and began to fall to the ground. The same is true of missiles fired by gunpowder weapons such as guns and cannons. Eventually, a bullet, shell, or cannonball slows down and falls to the ground.

FIRST STUDIES

The first person to study missiles was the Italian Niccolò Fontana Tartaglia. In 1537, he tried to figure out the path of a cannonball in the air.

This 1606 book shows the paths Tartaglia believed a cannonball followed, depending on the angle at which it was fired.

The ancient Greek philosopher Aristotle had said that a missile flew in a straight line before falling straight to the ground. Tartaglia agreed that a cannonball flew straight. However, he thought that it did not fall to the ground in a straight line. Tartaglia believed a cannonball followed a curved path.

GALILEO'S EXPERIMENT

In the early seventeenth century, the Italian scientist Galileo Galilei figured out a way to test the flight of a cannonball.

Range-Finding

How far a bullet, cannonball, or shell travels depends on a number of factors. The first is the angle at which it is launched. The second is the speed at which it leaves the barrel of a weapon. The third is gravity, which slows the missile down. As long as gunners know how far away a target is, they can calculate how to hit it.

A US Marine uses a range finder to measure the distance to a target. The range finder measures distance using a laser beam.

A shell leaves a US M198 howitzer during a firing exercise. A howitzer fires shells in a high arc at low speed.

Galileo covered a bronze ball with ink. He rolled it across a large sloping surface. The ball acted as a cannon ball acts in the air. It traveled forward for a time before slowing down and rolling toward the bottom of the slope. The ink traced the exact path followed by the ball.

The ball's path confirmed Tartaglia's theory. As a **projectile** slows down in the air, it falls toward the ground in a curve. This effect is caused by Earth's gravity, which pulls the projectile down. As the projectile slows down, the effect of gravity grows stronger.

HITTING THE TARGET

Galileo later figured out how to calculate the path of a missile. The path forms a curve called a parabola. This knowledge made it possible for gunners to hit targets more accurately. They know the weight of a shell and how fast it travels. They also measure the distance to the target. They use this information to figure out at which angle to set the barrels of their cannons so that gravity will slow the shell enough to make it fall on the target.

The Norden Bombsight

During World War II (1939–1945), the US Army Air Force used a device called a Norden bombsight. It aimed bombs from high altitude. When the bomber had a target in his sight, he pressed a release button. A simple computer used the airplane's height and speed to figure out the right position from which to drop the bomb to hit the target.

Smoke rises from explosions during a bombing raid on Germany during World War II. The British and Americans carried out thousands of similar raids during the war.

23

CODES IN WORLD WAR II

British and American mathematicians in World War II faced some of the most complicated codes used until that time. The Germans used machines to encode messages.

A German soldier keys a message into an Engima machine while another soldier writes down the cipher message.

Enigma was the most famous code machine of the war. The user typed a message on a keyboard. When a key was pressed, three **rotor** wheels moved inside the machine. The rotors made a letter light up on a display. That was the letter used in the cipher.

CHANGING SEQUENCE

The rotors in the Enigma machine changed each time a key was pressed, so the sequence of letters in the cipher appeared random. In fact, the sequence depended on the settings of the device at the start of the message. Operators used top secret codebooks to reset the machines. The rotors, wires, and other parts of the machine could all be changed. The machine had so many changing parts that the ciphers it created were impossible to break.

The coded message was sent wirelessly by a radio transmitter in Morse code. At its destination, it was picked up by a receiver and keyed into another Enigma machine. Because it had the same settings as the original machine, the second machine reproduced the original plaintext message.

THE FIRST MACHINES

In 1932, a French spy had learned about an early Enigma machine. It only had one rotor. Polish mathematicians broke the first Enigma codes. In 1939, the Germans added two more rotors to the machine. That made the code far more complex. The Germans believed the code was unbreakable.

Enigma Machine

The German engineer Arthur Scherbius built the Enigma machine. He sold it to the German Navy in 1926. The machine was complex. Not only did the operator reset the three rotors for each message, but the also reset rings of letters on each rotor and moved the wires that joined the rotors to the keyboard.

The Enigma machine was designed so that the operator could easily reset the three rotors (top of keyboard) and the wires that joined them to the keys.

A NEW DEVICE

British code breakers studied the work of the Polish mathematicians and used it to figure out a way to break the Enigma code. In 1943 the German High Command realized that Enigma had been cracked. They introduced the Lorenz machine. It was a far more complex version of the Enigma machine with 12 rotors. It could encrypt a message billions of ways. The Germans believed it could not be cracked. However, an operator made a mistake that allowed the Allies to figure out the codes.

The German Lorenz machine had twelve rotors. Each rotor had movable rings of letters. Lorenz could generate billions of possible ciphers for the same message.

ALLIED CODE MACHINES

The British and Americans had their own code machines during World War II. Britain's machine was called Typex. It was based on the design of the Enigma machine in the 1930s. It had seven rotors, so it was more complex than Enigma. The Americans developed a machine named the ECB Mark II or SIGABA. None of the codes generated by these devices was ever broken by the enemy.

A Japanese cruiser burns in June 1942. US ships attacked the Japanese Navy at Midway after decoded messages revealed the movements of the Japanese fleet.

JN-25

The Imperial Japanese Navy used book ciphers rather than machines. The Americans called the Japanese codebook JN-25. The book included more than 90,000 words. US code breakers noticed the repetition of formal phrases such as "your excellency." They used that information and a machine that counted the occurrences of characters to break the JN-25 cipher.

BREAKING THE ENIGMA CODE

At the start of World War II, Britain set up a secret center to break enemy codes. It was based at Bletchley Park in the middle of the country. The project was officially called the Government Code and Cipher School.

The British hired all sorts of people as code breakers. Many were math professors or graduates from top universities. Others were linguists, or people who studied languages. Some recruits were experts in **hieroglyphics** and other ancient scripts. The British also hired chess players and people who did crossword puzzles.

Bletchley Park was a large mansion in a quiet part of central England. Few people knew of its existence.

At its largest, Bletchley Park was home to more than 10,000 code breakers. They were divided into groups based in wooden huts. The mathematician Alan Turing led Hut 8. The hut was responsible for breaking the Enigma ciphers used by the German navy.

BREAKING ENIGMA

Turing invented an **electromechanical** device he called the Bombe. Using the Bombe, Turing and the chess player Hugh Alexander broke the Enigma codes. The British could now track the position of German **U-boats**, or submarines, in the Atlantic Ocean. The British also learned that Japan was preparing for war. The Germans, meanwhile, did not initially realize that their security had been broken.

THE BRAINS

Alan Turing (1912–1954) led the British code-breaking efforts. He was a mathematician and a computer pioneer. He came up with the idea for the Turing machine, an early type of computer, in 1936, and invented the Bombe during the war. Turing is seen as being the father of computer science.

Learning the position of German U-boats allowed Allied ships and aircraft to bomb them.

COLOSSUS VS. LORENZ

Bletchley Park was also home to the world's first programmable electronic computer. This machine, Colossus, helped crack codes from Lorenz cipher machines. The Lorenz code was used to send important information between high-ranking officers. The British had the chance to break the code when a German operator made an error. The operator sent the same message twice. The first message was in code, but the second message also included short forms of words. A code breaker named William Tutte studied the messages. He looked for patterns and repetitions in the cipher and figured out how the Lorenz machine worked.

After the war, British Prime Minister Winston Churchill destroyed all records of Bletchley Park and the work of the code breakers.

Breaking the Lorenz code gave the Allies a huge advantage. Now they could read German plans about troop movements and military strategy. US President Dwight D. Eisenhower later said that the code breakers had shortened World War II by at least two years.

A 30-YEAR SECRET

Security was tight at Bletchley Park. All the workers promised never to reveal their work. Not even their families knew what they had done. Details of Bletchley Park's wartime role only became known in the 1970s.

AERONAUTICS

Aeronautics is the science of flight. Pioneers of flight used math to figure out how to get a heavy machine off the ground and keep it in the air.

Early scientists studied flight by watching birds. Ancient Egyptian texts include details about how birds fly. In Europe in the late fifteenth century, the artist and inventor Leonardo da Vinci also studied birds. He used his observations to design the first manned flying machines. His plan for an "ornithopter" had wings that were flapped by a pilot moving his arms. Da Vinci also designed a helicopter that had a rotating screw like a modern **propeller**. Da Vinci never built his machines, but modern scientists have learned that they would never had been able to fly. They required far more energy to fly than a pilot could generate.

The large wings of Leonardo da Vinci's ornithopter would have met too much air resistance for a pilot to be able to flap them.

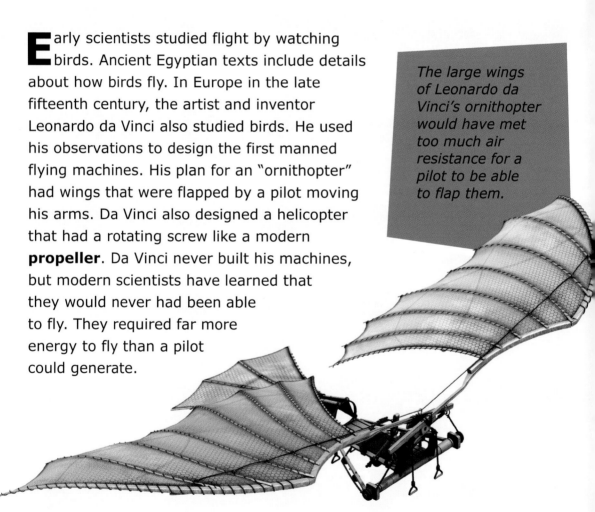

FOUR FORCES

In the early nineteenth century, a British engineer named George Cayley began the first scientific study of **aviation**. He identified the four forces involved in flight as thrust, drag, lift, and weight. Thrust, or forward motion, helped an aircraft to overcome drag, or air resistance. Lift was the force that lifted an aircraft into the air. To do this, it had to overcome the force of gravity that acted on the aircraft's weight. Cayley calculated an aircraft design that would be likely to fly.

Creating Lift

The key to creating lift is the shape of the wing. A wing has a flat underside but a curved upper side. As a wing moves through the air, air traveling over the wing has farther to travel than air passing beneath it. This creates lower air pressure above the wing, which causes the wing to rise upward, creating lift.

*The French inventor Otto Lilienthal flies a **glider** in 1895. The two wings create a larger surface area than one single wing and provide more lift.*

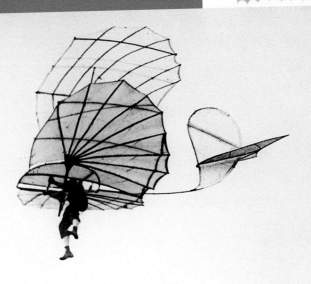

In 1804 Cayley built a glider that set the shape of nearly all airplanes in the future. It had a long body with wings near the middle. Its vertical tail had horizontal fins to make the aircraft more stable. A glider is so light that it is lifted into the air by the wind. Once it is airborne, it is supported by rising currents of warm air known as thermals.

A model of a fighter airplane is tested in a wind tunnel before World War II. The bent wings of the airplane allowed space for it to carry a bomb load.

POWERED FLIGHT

Other scientists developed Cayley's work. They used wind tunnels to study how air interacts with solid objects. The French inventor Otto Lilienthal experimented with gliders. He figured out that thin, curved wings would produce high lift and low drag. In 1903, Orville and Wilbur Wright used this knowledge to build the first powered airplane.

The Wright Brothers' airplane was powered by a propeller engine. That was the case for all airplanes until 1939, when the Heinkel He 178 became the first jet airplane. It flew by forcing air through a spinning **turbine**. In June 1944, the Germans introduced the Me 262. It was the world's first jet fighter.

Twin jet engines gave the Me 262 a top speed of 560 miles (900 kilometers) per hour.

THE BRAINS

Willy Messerschmitt (1898–1978) was a German engineer who made his name during World War II. He designed the Bf 109, the most important fighter plane of the German air force, or Luftwaffe. Later in the war, he also designed the Me 262, the world's first jet fighter. The Me 262 had wings that pointed backward, which helped it to achieve high speeds.

LOGISTICS

Military logistics is the name given to the process of moving troops and supplies. Its name comes from the Greek word *logistikos*, which means "skilled in calculating."

The first important figure in military logistics was a Frenchman named Michel le Tellier. In the late seventeenth century, Le Tellier created a professional army in France. He calculated how much ammunition and food each soldier needed so that he could figure out how many supplies the army needed. To make the process smoother, he wrote standard agreements for suppliers to provide food or equipment quickly for a set cost. Tellier also introduced supply depots near the front line. They enabled **provisions** to reach soldiers quickly.

The British built a railroad to supply its soldiers at Balaclava in the Crimea during the Crimean War (1853–1856). The rail cars were pulled by horses.

This bridge was built by Union engineers in the Civil War to make the rail line usable again after the bridge was destroyed by Confederates.

The American Civil War

During the Civil War, the Union controlled almost three-quarters of all railroads. Lacking railroads meant the Confederates could not supply their armies. Late in the war, this became a serious disadvantage. In 1865, the inability to move supplies was an important factor in the Confederate defeat.

RAIL TRANSPORTATION

For centuries, armies used horse-drawn transport to move supplies. But when the steam locomotive was invented in the middle of the nineteenth century, it became possible to move supplies by railroad. During the Crimean War, the British Army built a special railroad line to supply frontline troops.

WORLD WAR I

In World War I, both sides built lines of trenches in northern France and Belgium. This was called the Western Front, and it did not move far for most of the conflict. The conflict was fought on a huge scale, involving millions of soldiers. In just one battle in 1918, for example, US artillery units fired more than 800,000 shells. Both sides needed to move large amounts of ammunition and other supplies to the front lines

Both sides built permanent railroads to move supplies. They also built roads. World War I was the first conflict in which motor vehicles such as trucks played a major role in moving supplies. However, in parts of the Western Front that had been badly shelled, the ground was too rough for trucks to be used. Armies there used horses to pull supply wagons through the mud and among shell craters.

Soldiers at a US supply depot in France in World War I fill cans with gasoline from tankers for use in trucks and tanks.

A Japanese cargo ship sinks after being hit by a US submarine in the Pacific Ocean.

Planning Ahead

People who organize military supplies are called quartermasters. They use statistics to figure out how many supplies they need. Modern military forces need so much hardware, ammunition, fuel, and food that it is impossible to make it from scratch if a conflict begins. The US Navy, for example, tries to calculate the likelihood of a major incident at sea. That helps it figure out how much fuel to order and store.

WORLD WAR II

Logistics were more difficult in World War II. The United States, Britain, and their allies fought the Germans and their allies. Britain depended on food and military equipment from the United States. German submarines tried to sink supply ships crossing the Atlantic Ocean. The Allies used warships, aircraft, and **radar** to protect them. Japan also depended on imported supplies. US Navy submarines sank many Japanese ships in the Pacific Ocean. The lack of imported supplies severely damaged Japan's economy.

STATISTICS AND RECORDS

In the past, most armies kept few statistics, or detailed mathematical facts, about their soldiers. Since the nineteenth century, statistics have become key to warfare.

In the US Civil War, both sides kept detailed records. The Union and Confederate armies kept records of all soldiers who joined up. They also noted any wounds the soldiers suffered. They recorded if soldiers were killed or when they left the army. In 1864, the Union began gathering its war records in *The War of the Rebellion: Official Records of the Civil War*.

The German city of Nuremberg lies in ruins in World War II. Keeping records of damage to property helps to organize and pay for rebuilding work after a war.

From 1865 this also included Confederate figures. The completed OR, as the work is known, filled 127 volumes.

WORLD WAR I

In World War I, both sides kept detailed information about their soldiers. In the huge battles on the Western Front, generals quickly knew how many men were killed or wounded, even if the bodies were never found. It also became possible for people at home to find out quickly if someone had died.

Dog Tags

Dog tags were introduced by the US Army in 1906. All US soldiers wore them by 1913. The metal tags were worn around the neck and were used to identify dead or wounded soldiers. Tags listed key information such as a soldier's name and military serial number. They also included medical information such as blood type. The tags were usually worn in identical pairs. If a soldier was killed, one tag was removed so his death could be reported. The other stayed with the body so it could be identified.

Soldiers used rubber silencers so their dog tags did not tap together and give away the soldier's position.

WORLD WAR II

In World War II, statistics played a key role in the air war. Both sides bombed military, civilian, and industrial targets of the other side. Airplanes took photographs of the damage. Analysts used the photographs to try to figure out how much damage a bombing attack had caused. This helped planners know whether or not to attack a target for a second time.

During World War II, bombing raids caused civilian casualties as well as damage to property, like this destroyed railroad station in London.

ANALYSIS OF WARS

From the late 1940s the mathematician Lewis Fry Richardson began to analyze wars. Richardson used math to try to figure out why wars start. He argued that **arms races** increased the chances of war. Richardson gathered his data in *Statistics of Deadly Quarrels*.

Richardson analyzed wars between 1809 and 1949 and grouped them according to the number of casualties. Richardson used **probability theory** to try to predict which countries might go to war. He hoped to help people to come up with ways to avoid future wars.

Wars continue to break out, however. Modern warfare relies on computers and complex smart weapons. This means math is likely to remain at the heart of warfare.

SCIENCE FILE

Casualty Figures

Casualty figures for wars include both military personnel and civilians. The relationship between them is called the civilian casualty ratio. Before the twentieth century, about the same number of soldiers and civilians died, so the ratio was about 50 percent. During World War II, both sides bombed population centers. The ratio rose to 70 percent civilians killed. In more recent conflicts in Afghanistan and the Middle East, civilians were often caught up in the fighting. The civilian casualty ratio has risen as high as 90 percent.

A war cemetery from World War I in France. The first war cemeteries were created during the American Civil War.

TIMELINE

c. 1900–1500 BCE   Early attempts at hidden communication using ciphers are made using hieroglyphs in the Old Kingdom of Egypt and on clay tablets found in Mesopotamia.

c. 700 BCE   The Spartans invent the scytale, a strip of parchment that wrapped around a rod to reveal secret military messages.

c. 200 BCE   The Polybius Square, a grid of letters used for encrypting signals, is invented in ancient Greece.

c. 100 BCE   The monoalphabetic Caesar cipher is developed in the Roman Empire.

c. 800   The Arab mathematician Al-Kindi shows how frequency analysis can be used to break ciphers.

1553   Giovan Battista Bellaso develops a powerful polyalphabetic cipher. It is widely known as the Vigenère cipher.

1799   British engineer George Cayley identifies the aerodynamic forces of flight.

1813   Topographical "terrain intelligence" is used to plan troop formations in the Prussian defeat of Napoleon at Silesia.

1844   Samuel Morse demonstrates his electric telegraph to Congress, tapping out the message "What hath God wrought" in what becomes known as Morse code.

1863	Prussian military officer Friedrich Kasiski publishes *Die Geheimschriften und die Dechiffrir-Kunst* ("Secret Writing and the Art of Deciphering"), the first major work on cryptography. It includes a method for decoding the Vigenère cipher that became known as the Kasiski Examination.
1918	German mathematician and engineer Arthur Scherbius patents the Enigma rotary cipher machine. The machines are adopted by the German military in 1926.
1939	Working for British Intelligence at Bletchley Park, British mathematician Alan Turing designs an electromechanical machine called the Bombe, capable of breaking any cipher produced by the German Enigma machines.
1942	In a feat of reverse-engineering, code breakers at Bletchley Park work out the complete logical structure of the German Lorenz cipher machines.
1960	Lewis Fry Richardson publishes *Statistics of Deadly Quarrels*, a mathematical analysis of every military conflict from 1809 to 1949.
2000	The Shuttle Radar Topography Mission produces a three-dimensional terrain map of 80 percent of the world's land surface. The maps are used by US military forces.

GLOSSARY

arms races: periods of tension when two or more countries try to manufacture more powerful weapons than their enemies

artillery: large guns such as cannons

aviation: the design, construction, and operation of aircraft

climate: the usual weather conditions in a particular region

electromechanical: describes a device with moving parts that is operated by electricity

elevation: the height of something above a particular level, such as the ground

geared: using toothed wheels that fit into other wheels as a way to transfer energy in a machine

glider: a light aircraft that flies without an engine

hieroglyphics: a type of picture writing used in ancient Egypt

keyword: a word or sequence of letters that sets the key for creating or decrypting a coded message

navigation: the process of planning and following a route

probability theory: a branch of mathematics that tries to calculate the chances of events occurring

projectile: a missile designed to be fired from a gun

propeller: a turning blade that propels a ship or aircraft

provisions: food, drink, and other supplies

radar: short for radio detection and ranging, a system for locating objects by bouncing radio waves off them

rotor: a group of rotating blades

surveyors: people who carefully study and measure features in the landscape

turbine: a machine in which a rotor wheel is made to revolve by fast moving water or air to produce power

U-boats: English for *Unterseeboots*, which is German for "submarines"

FURTHER RESOURCES

Books

Barber, Nicola. *Who Broke the Wartime Codes?* Chicago: Heinemann Library, 2014.

Demuth, Patricia Brennan. *Who Was Galileo?* New York: Grosset and Dunlap, 2015.

Gurstelle, William. *Backyard Ballistics: Build Potato Cannons, Paper Match Rockets, Cincinnati Fire Kites, Tennis Ball Mortars, and More Dynamite Devices*. Chicago: Chicago Review Press, 2012.

Nagelhout, Ryan. *Alan Turing: Master of Cracking Codes.* New York: PowerKids Press, 2016.

Orr, Tamra. *The Railroad and the Civil War*. Hockessin, Del: Mitchell Lane Publishers, 2013.

Websites

Bletchley Park
**http://www.historylearningsite
.co.uk/world-war-two/world
-war-two-in-western-europe
/code-breaking-at-bletchley
-park/bletchley-park/**

Compare War Statistics
http://wars.findthedata.com/

Enigma
**http://www.bbc.co.uk/history
/topics/enigma**

George Cayley
**http://spartacus-educational
.com/SCIcayley.htm**

How Airplanes Work
**http://science.howstuffworks
.com/transport/flight/modern
/airplanes.htm**

Who Was Alan Turing?
**http://www.bbc.co.uk/timelines
/z8bgr82**

INDEX